How to Avoid Speaking

How to Avoid Speaking

Jaimee Hills

WAYWISER

First published in 2015 by

THE WAYWISER PRESS

Christmas Cottage, Church Enstone, Chipping Norton, Oxon OX7 4NN, UK
P.O. Box 6205, Baltimore, MD 21206, USA
http://waywiser-press.com

Editor-in-Chief
Philip Hoy

Senior American Editor
Joseph Harrison

Associate Editors
Dora Malech | Eric McHenry | V. Penelope Pelizzon | Clive Watkins
Greg Williamson | Matthew Yorke

Copyright © Jaimee Hills, 2015

The right of Jaimee Hills to be identified as the author of this work
has been asserted by her in accordance with the
Copyright, Designs and Patents Act of 1988.

All rights reserved

A CIP catalogue record for this book is available from the British Library

ISBN 978-1-904130-84-0

Printed and bound by
T. J. International Ltd., Padstow, Cornwall, PL28 8RW

For G, Z, & C

Acknowledgments

The author wishes to thank the editors of the following journals in whose pages these poems (or previous versions of them) first appeared: *Best New Poets 2006*: "Still Life"; *Blackbird*: "On S" appearing as "Lesson on the Letter S"; *Confrontation Magazine*: "Battle of the Cricket" and "Discerning Sound"; *Country Dog Review*: "Synaesthesia"; *Drunken Boat*: "Derrida Eats a Dorito"; *Gargoyle*: "Tonight the Character of Death Will Be Played by Brad Pitt"; *The Kennesaw Review*: "Harpy" and "Eurydice"; *Measure*: "Doll Coffins"; *Poemeleon*: "Albanian Virgin"; *Poetry Northwest*: "Lavender Mist"; *Red Paint Hill*: "Lo Lee Ta"; *RHINO*: "The Fascist Poem"; *Sewanee Theological Review*: "Emaciated Muse"; *TAB*: "Lullaby"; *Unsplendid*: "The Bar" and "Graven Image"; *The Vocabula Review*: "Nothing Rhymes with Gitmo" and "My Sexist Thesaurus"; *Waccamaw*: "Chlamydia" and "Echo and Narcissus."

The author gratefully acknowledges the assistance of the MFA program at UNC-Greensboro, the Johns Hopkins University Writing Seminars program, the Vermont Studio Center, the Sewanee Writers' Conference, and all those involved in bringing to fruition this book at Waywiser Press.

The author also wishes to thank John and Betty Hills, Gerry Canavan, Zoey Hills Canavan, Connor Hills Canavan, teachers/mentors John Irwin, Greg Williamson, Isaac Cates, Dave Smith, Fred Chappell, Julia Johnson, Stuart Dischell, Van Jordan, the incomparable "Women's Group" at UNCG, contest judge Anthony Thwaite, cover artist Cecilia Paredes, Barbara Hamby, and careful readers, Jennie Thompson and Jennifer Whitaker, who all contributed to the existence of this book.

Contents

FOREWORD BY ANTHONY THWAITE   11

I

Synaesthesia   15
Chlamydia   16
Lullaby   17
Discerning Sound   18
Birds   19
Saxifrage Is My Flower that Splits the Rocks   20
True Knot   21
Lavender Mist   22
Sprung   23
Somber   24
Fallen   25
Wonder   26
Radiance   27
The Oyster   28
How to Avoid Speaking   29

II

On S   35
Lo Lee Ta   36
Andy Warhol's Wig   38
On X-Rays   39
On M   40
Wonder Woman's Resumé   41
Frida Kahlo's Eyebrows   42
On J   43
On Q-Tips   44
On D   45
On F   46
On Z   47

III

Derrida Eats a Dorito	51
Nothing Rhymes with Gitmo	52
Keys to the Kingdom	53
Albanian Virgin	54
The Snows of Kilimanjaro Are Melting	55
Windmills	56
Echo and Narcissus	57
Lust	60
Couple On Display	61
On Beauty	62
30-Second Spot	63
Poet as Anticapitalist	64

IV

Tonight the Character of Death Will Be Played by Brad Pitt	69
The Bar	70
Aubade for Resusci-Annie	71
Doll Coffins	72
The Fascist Poem	73
Ode to Fear	74
Battle of the Cricket	75
Textbook Smile	76
Graven Image	77
Noli Me Tangere	78
Eurydice	80
My Sexist Thesaurus	81
Emaciated Muse	82
Harpy	83
Still Life	84
NOTES	87
A NOTE ABOUT THE AUTHOR	89
A NOTE ABOUT THE ANTHONY HECHT POETRY PRIZE	91

Foreword by Anthony Thwaite

I don't think I have ever before judged a poetry competition in which I found myself laughing aloud. That I did so with *How to Avoid Speaking* is one measure of the book's distinction. I exclaimed ("Wow!") and giggled, as well as laughing. Jaimee Hills is enviably gifted, exuberantly ingenious, smilingly audacious.

Her language is, by turns, baroque, rococo, and precisely "contemporary" (whatever that means). And it isn't only the language that is inventive and provocative, so is the syntax. She plays with constructions as well as with idioms and with vocabulary, and as you read you have to keep your wits about you, as she does.

The well-made poem seems widely out of fashion in America, as it is in Britain. In their different ways, W. H. Auden, Anthony Hecht (of course), Richard Wilbur, Howard Nemerov, Randall Jarrell produced well-made poems. Amy Clampitt is another example, perhaps more like the poet of *How to Avoid Speaking*. In Britain, in their different ways, Philip Larkin and James Fenton are exemplars of the well-made poem, masters of style. Indeed, some might judge Jaimee Hills's poems as being exercises in style. They are not just that, though they are very stylish.

Stylishness can carry with it a side-effect: obscurity. Jaimee Hills never strikes me as being ostentatiously or wilfully obscure. She means what she says. One can always find a substantial thread of meaning (and often a great deal more than that) in each poem. Not, I think, since William Empson in the late 1920s and 1930s has there been such a nimble trickster of a poet, and yet *How to Avoid Speaking* is not in the least Empsonian.

In among all the cleverness and stylishness, there is real feeling: "True Knot", "Radiance", "Doll Coffins". But open the collection wherever you like and you will almost certainly be drawn into Jaimee Hills's strange and seductive world. The very first poem, "Synaesthesia", assured me immediately that I was in safe hands: I passed it to a friend, a good poet who happened to call in while I was reading, and he gave it back to me with the words: "I think this is your poet". He turned out to be right.

Foreword by Anthony Thwaite

This is the tenth winner of the Anthony Hecht Poetry Prize, and it is a collection I was very glad to find.

I

Synaesthesia

Bonnard could see the sunset in a peach,
a pomegranate in a cheek. The flesh
of nudes broke sunlight into paint daubs; each
dull shadow grew hydrangea from a brush,
worn out, splayed like an orange trumpet blare.
Hear the word that is *orange*, colored sweet,
the timbre of a peel pulled from its meat
like diving in the sunlit water's glare.

To infants, armchairs have a look of anger,
or maybe chirping birds sound light, the fear
in Mama's *no* is tinged with a red clang—
before our senses define, before our language
forms what's practical, before you hear
the shadow whisper, *All of this is wrong.*

Chlamydia

Like *cellar door*,
Chlamydia.
There's melody cloaked in the malady.
Forget the cinderblocks, the grimy ground
behind the words, like the brutality
of the rain. Hear its lovely drum, the sound
Chlamydia
caught in the downpour.

Like clematis,
Chlamydia,
a clitoris by any other name.
The name as sweet might mean a creeping flower,
petal-clad, wearing the silky plume
of traveler's joy, snowdrift, virgin's bower,
chlamydia,
or satin curls.

Like Clytemnestra,
Chlamydia
(whose mother Leda caught it from a swan).
It ought to be the color tangerine,
a lightning storm, a high-class salon,
this parasite who should have been a queen,
Chlamydia,
another Cleopatra.

Like Fragonard,
Chlamydia.
In a French Rococo garden, light and gaudy,
it drapes a woman on a swing mid-swoop
as a man kneels below her skirt—both bawdy
in their powdered wigs, her pose, his gape.
Chlamydia
should swap with *fulgid*.

Lullaby

On a willow bough, an owl *who*s.
The byway bellows below.
Eely willows, lilies, and bluebells
yoyo a ballet.

Yells well up—a baby bawls
in a web of blue and yellow.
The bluebells bob like wallabies.
The lilies lap his elbow.

Lulling him a lullaby,
the willow lowly bows.
The wily lilies bully while
the willable bluebells obey.

The baby boy lies ill. The willow
sways bye-bye. The lilies
lie about their alibi.
The loyal bluebells bail.

The baby blows away. The bellows
allay. The willow wails
and wobbles while a yellow owl
eye allows it all.

Discerning Sound

That twig snap expresses the weight of a foot. Certainly
there's a train in the distance. Through the curtain
I see two young deer ghost out of the skirt

of the woods. In this moment the leaves sound eloquent.
There's a flute in the trees, or a song of a yellow
bird. That continual far off thud will tell

that a man punches the wall in the other room—but actually
clothes stir in the dryer. Outside, sounds askew,
my neighbors argue. Echoes fall slack

through the stairwell ringing through the brass fixtures
of the foyer. Their yells turn to fists and mix
with the bird's whistle. An inhuman trick.

At play in the yard, children scream most afternoons.
Today too, they punctuate the air with laughter.
But who could tell the difference if

they were dying? My neighbors have ceased. I orient
myself to believe that next door a murder story
takes shape. The floor creaks. No, a snore
whistles. The flute whistles. The bird.

Birds

Diamond dove, masked finfoot, tundra swan,
wandering tattler, splendid fairy-wren,
chestnut-backed jewel-babbler, nightingale,
snail kite, rufous-headed pygmy-tyrant,
yellow-bellied sapsucker, spike-heeled lark,
horned screamer, greater necklaced laughingthrush,
squirrel cuckoo, harlequin duck, anhinga, sun grebe,
cinnamon tanager, noisy friarbird,
black-fronted nun bird, speckled chachalaca,
painted bunting, little spotted kiwi,
lizard buzzard, long-wattled umbrellabird,
yellow-faced honeyeater, ovenbird,
star-throated antwren, topaz-frilled coquette,
dead sea sparrow, sooty albatross,
sociable weaver, firewood-gatherer,
rusty-cheeked scimitar-babbler, zebra finch,
helmeted manakin, apostlebird,
spectacled monarch, emerald toucanet,
violet sabrewing, pied butcherbird,
dark chanting goshawk, red-necked avocet,
tawny frogmouth, secretary bird,
northern flicker, fan-tailed berrypecker,
emperor penguin, sapphire-rumped parrotlet,
boat-billed heron, hermit hummingbird,
chimney swift, antenna satinbird,
harpy eagle, golden whistler, brambling,
violet-fronted brilliant, purple swamphen,
silvereye, pink pigeon, rosy-faced lovebird.

Saxifrage Is My Flower that Splits the Rocks

(after William Carlos Williams)

Willow aster is my rolling star that shoots—then wilts.
Wallflower is my stake against a swarm of dancers, waltzing.
Anemone is my breeze, the daughter of the wind and a
    weathervane.

Nasturtium is my flower that can twist the nose.
Marigold is my ocean holding little golden calamari.
Dandelion is my lion's tooth that crumbles into dandruff.

Heather is my broom that tickles wastelands with a feather.
Gladiolus is my cluster of swords for when I need defending.
Geranium is my paper crane's bill that unbirdly folds in front of
    strangers.

Peony is my physician with a thin green stethoscope.
Poppy is my swollen flower whose red bud is a lollypop.
Rosemary is my dew of the sea, which is wet everywhere.

Heliotrope is my key that turns the sun like a helicopter.
Tulip is my winding gauze worn as a turban.
Sweet William is my bunch pink, my punch drink, my wishing
    helmet.

True Knot

True knots never bind, but threaten.
Tenderly I expected you,
outlier burst from my loamed brain,
rainslick, cherubic pink of Titian,

not the orchid you flowered into,
tousled, blue, and taciturn.
Turnip, tell me you understand
standoffs with eternity:

spot on the ceiling in a tailspin,
spine-curved doctors huddle your body,
dying, as they avert fiasco,
coax your urgent rasp with silver.

You found a loophole to slip through,
roughly speaking, an acrobat.
Bated mammal, you discover
vernix, torsion, the joy of air,

your name, typewritten, escaping limbo,
bound to my heart, a reservoir.

Lavender Mist

(Pollock, 1950)

Violence. Airily, this mist
veils a field of lavender.
Delay yourself. The colors run
diluvial; daylilies stir.
                This mist
drives a vivid fist to the face,
unravels aurora – scimitars
strike tiny needles on your cheek,
a violet splatter. Nerve burst. Stars.
                This mist,
a vernal taste of endive, olive,
the universe enveloped in
the scent of lavender, the sound
of lavender, the void, the din.
                This mist,
the divine inkblot of *voilà*;
ardor, villain, vandal, whatever
overruns your mind this moment
as the sun glints in the river.

Sprung

Ubiquitous sperm
in lime dust on the windshields,
color of inchworm,
on sidewalks seething,
I despise you most of all.
Leave. Leave me breathing.

All the jerks are out
today in the parks, kissing.
They pucker. They pout.
They watch propellers
twirl from trees, sniff buttercups,
and read bestsellers.

The wind, your lover,
played with my hair and planted
small seeds all over
as I ducked the trees
with their hanging genitals
and began to wheeze.

As the world breaks loose,
a lemon shock fills my nose.
I blink grapefruit juice.
Hush bees! You indict
the flowers? The azaleas
all freaked out last night.

Somber

Twice a year, the street became the sky.
The people held their breath. The army jeep
made clouds fan out from its slick canister
enveloping the street, the yards, in mist—
a miracle that helped us win the war.

Volatile, I am a shy ancestor
of such a rain. My father chased the dust
HARMLESS TO HUMANS, chased the sinister
spray each mosquito season, touched the weep,
the plume of poison, summer sprinkler, play.

Fallen

A moose in the field   keeps failing. The fallen
leaves are chasing   a creature of chills.
A painter probes   an empty park bench.
The fox on the hill   hunted and hunting
ducks in the shadows   in the dark distance.
A reaper wrestles   a metal rake
that speaks in slices   its fingers scraping.
The red-breasted snipe   bleeding and bulleted
ebbs from an elm   into the earth bones.

A helicopter's   heard overhead.
At the gas station   a gunshot digresses—
backfire, breaking   glass, the burst
of rockets? The gust   of gas and the gloss
of shopping bags   stir in the stream.
A touch, a trace   in the troposphere.
A white envelope   blows westward, wasted.

Wonder

Startled at the popping, clinking spoons,
the sound of steam inside its steel cocoons,
she said, *What's that?* and guessed it was a ghost
or some intruder prowling, jangling pipes.

A clunky thief like that, louder than most,
might break in through the basement afternoons
to steal the heat, stow it inside balloons.
Winters are hard on burglars. It's the frost.

I barely notice now. No ghost-crook swipes
the heat, wrecks the quiet, stirs the drapes.
The antique heating system's errant noise
begins with a low rasp, then soon erupts
like an idea into the clang and taps
of a heatsong. Isn't that what a ghost is?

Radiance

To C (7 weeks old)

Beautiful plastic clings to the window,
the outside world an innuendo
of sunrise, crackling through gemstones. Squint
and a glass master fashioned the tinted
drink of amber, honey, cognac—
mosaic of sea glass, primordial stone.

You keep craning your head, clumsily,
lifting its heft up to get a glimpse.
New consciousness ignites your face:
your smile calculates the cosmos,
your eyes, blue still, small astrolabes.
What is it you see, sweetie babes?

The Oyster

At first, it seemed the world was like an oyster
served on a silver platter, bed of pearls,
soft flesh on the half shell, the alabaster
dish of Venus, paired with a good white wine.
The captive sea might taste like stone, metallic,
or sweet as melon, dressed with parsley, swirls
of butter, lemon juice, a touch of garlic.
You'd simply ring the dinner bell and dine.

In fact, the oyster's risky, razor-sharp,
to be shucked with a knife at the hinge in its back. Unease
fills the deep breath you take before you gulp
the entire thing alive. Forget the reckless
little skull inside its little sea
that wears the fishbowl treasure like a tease.
That cloistered pearl of opportunity
takes time, from agitating grit to necklace.

How to Avoid Speaking

I

If comments that tend to kill
a conversation curl up in your tongue's lap,
be beautiful, rude, haughty, and dress well.
As more loquacious ladies
talk Michelangelo, you come and go,
iceberg aloof, in your own private hades.

If the partiers are quiet,
let the wallpaper buzz. Become a puzzle,
mum by the mums and let the roses riot.
The brook will babble, headstrong.
Keep it tacit. Chorus the trickling, dulcet
drip, drip, drip…as the faucet makes a birdsong.

II

As the faucet makes a birdsong,
a fingertip will line a crystal glass lip
and echo like a microphone. If heard wrong,
or say, a fork should slip
your grasp and cling a champagne glass, that ding
will hone a crowd's attention. Make a quip.

Though you'll wonder how to be bubbly.
Simply blush. No speech. Keep it hush-hush.
Remember the ghost behind you speaks, the doubling
foe through the microphone.
The crowd, take heart, is in their underwear
but you're not bare. Why didn't you join in the fun?

How to Avoid Speaking

III

Why don't you join in the funnel
of sound and shout? Once the words land, then sprout
like woolly buggers in the ear canal,
once the wave is caught,
they won't return to your possession, but glint
bright as a dying fish, a fleeting thought.

Undiscover fire.
Uninvent the light bulb. Your potentials,
their nebulous multiplicity, will soar
beyond you, flitting outwards,
where language won't suffice. *Just* words. Think twice
before they fly from you, uncautious birds.

IV

From you, incautious birds
seek rhapsody, a bit of gingersnap,
sugar, spice, but nothing that a curtsy
might imply. Sedate,
buttoned up, cute as a button, mute,
you're bottled up, about to detonate.

Your soft voice, muffled snow pure,
airy as cotton candy, makes a pink sand
that bleeds the tongue. The mind is never demure.
There is, inside the skull,
a raging sea. If you are the lull in the eye
of the storm, there is a storm inside the lull.

How to Avoid Speaking

V

Inside the lullaby's note,
hear the hush. Born sheepish, in the year
of the goat, voice quiet, kenneled in your throat,
you bleat. Your small mouth coos.
Don't answer phones, prefer the sticks and stones,
to cliques and clones, syntax and tongues, which bruise

the memory. Shush. Don't
say uncle. Affirm nothing. In the skirmish
of noise, chisel your words to a fine point.
Be secretive. Withdrawn.
No one will know you hail from a clan of baboons.
Be secretive. Wear this penchant like a crown.

VI

Pinching like a crown,
the hew of a dull chat. That "How are you?"
is much too philosophical. Smile. Frown.
Perform your repertoire
of mime, feign narcolepsy, suck a lime,
tuck sound behind your useless uvula.

Express abstractly. Splash
paint across a canvas. Write down words meant
to be spoken on paper. Tell no one for weeks and stash
them in your pocket. Don't mention
why you linger, drawn, when you chance upon
a fire. Those burning whispers command attention.

VII

Whispers command attention,
give weight to the pin drop, compel your strain.
Your cloak-and-dagger ways create dimension,
mystery, but the twinge
of your sweet nothings (snap of the clam shell)
may be tart, curt, gutting like a ninja.

Inside a cutting remark,
terror and obscurity hold hands, dance
to invoke Dea Tacita, oligarch
of silence and bone chill
while the blunt heart murmurs, ventriloquent,
Hold your tongue, those comments, that tentacle.

II

On S

S is for sin. I knew what we were in for.
How could we exist without an exit?

He called me his apostrophe, a *she*, his little rib.
What soul? What self? I wanted to be singular.

In the beginning, there was light, but it was slight,
a soft wan-colored swan, a shallow lake to slake

our thirsty throats, an often hallow place
with susurrating psalms in the palm-fronds.

But a slow hiss announced itself.
The windswept willows wept. At thirty,

my possessive ex and I were fruitful,
peaking naked, multiplied our sex. But soon,

his low snaked tongue, in speaking, forked
our sour sons, our daughter and myself with words

of swords and I returned, both cursed and cured,
ears seared with newfound knowledge,

turned our laughter into slaughter.

Lo Lee Ta

L is for lover—isn't that the sick idea?
Wrong word, a world of wrong I'm over.
Slick ideal since lost. I'm pulp,
lost in the haze of a wet hazel sap, the welt
and slap of that warped princedom by the sea.

You stole my sole chance at its castle, just a pup
when you picked me, pickled slink. I shield
the seal of a caste of prey and sink
beneath your drive, your drivel, shied simply
like a flower's carpel. Carpe filia!

Hebephilia, the name culled for your infection.
My slender wrist was never a coy sender
of signals, no finch's beak full of inflection.
No cunning in the snap of my bubble gum.
Forget I sat on your lap. Surmise my glum shrug.

I flinch at how a pallid cheekbone cued
your poison. You paid my whines with sundaes
that cloy. Dolly, bleak little toy. Lola in slacks.
Pockets with sacks of lost minutes. A packet
of should-haves, slipped from my skirt placket.

Vile one. Do you vie for a heart or a flavor
to crawl on your tongue? What favor will slake
you? What stuck in my craw? For pity's sake,
I want to be a bell unrung, a clock
with no need for the cock or its crow.

To loll on a sofa, a bold dangler of limbs
without the danger of inciting a look. I lumber
a quilt of moments to burn in hell with every *he*.
Old slobs. Lecher, weld anguish with gold.
Usher me into jade. Languish into umber.

Lo Lee Ta

Wed me off to a lusher god. Bridle and bind me,
bride of wit with the long eyelashes. You're blind
to my wilt, my ashes. I grow into weed. Unhinged,
I grow into growl, and quit that welled-up note
that sobs for future. I'll be gone, singled and singed.

Andy Warhol's Wig

(née Warhola)

A woman threw my wig, a flurried silver ballerina,
down the stair to goad me. My god! She caused a stir.
Shot again, hunted, amazed she could gin up
that maze of memory, tiny pin of pain,
a punch to the paunch of my gut, a bluster
of wind. I paled like a marble baluster.
A is for Andy, my red pen pled, rattled
as a bell chimer's hand. A for abhorrent.

I turn haunted, wary of wry wig stealers.
I've known a tainted, aqua-tinted chimera.
Marilyn—we are in awe. We, America,
theists and atheists, drinkers of Coca-Cola,
all own a little piece of you. I am floating now,
in that small gulf between a person and persona.

On X-Rays

> "I know how they'll remember me: 'Here lies Marilyn Monroe, 34-24-36.'"

X is for Xanadu, that's me, a damsel
with-a-dulcimer-vision-in-a-dream. Sex

symbol in my day. A thing. Now dead. My chest
x-ray is up for auction. A clear example of ample

breasts. Purchase my pelvic exam. What I am
is triple X. I posed exposed, but not always undressed.

Glammed up, I stood on the x, went with the flux, blew
kisses. But they even make you act with the damn

flu. I read *Ulysses,* yet they hexed me with questions.
Do I wear underwear? Heed my words. Yes, I do.

Pester me. If I had to be a symbol of anything,
I'd rather it be sex than pirates or toxic waste.

Many things, like pomegranate seeds, will make you sexed.
Like Vicky, Bobbie, Dusky, Sugar, Lorelei, Cherie. Like Marilyn.

Your Maxim girl, looking for a heart to maim. Part hoax.
X-Acto nose-jobbed, bleached. Xeroxed and xanaxed.

A vixen. An apex. One of many foxes. One of many
foes. What should I say to such an ape? Grab your latex.

Honey, don't be late.

On M

> "No guilt, no mischief, no malignity, no misery, can be found comparable to mine." – the Monster (*Frankenstein*)

M is for mask. I ask, dear maker, for a form
that will not ache. A model in papier-mâché.

Instead you made me bone and marrow with an arrow
through the heart—not man, but an it. Dashed.

All that I see is utterly other to what I seem.
I mutter in my mummy bloom, my claim to matter.

Free of an old mold, no mother, unnourished
by milk. Bring the torches. Char me. Mash me.

Charm me. My ilk can never turn to ash.
My somber look can sober drunks and surely

stop you in your tracks. I march and stomp
about with a sad arch to my sad back.

How does one decide to mump a face up?
Domes for cheeks, a chip on a shoulder, chimp

parts soldered here and there. I smoldered with clamps
on the nubs of my neck, transformed from numb to warm,

hearing electric claps crackle through each seam. What hell—
my mind a disembodied war like the sea inside a shell.

Wonder Woman's Resumé

Wise as Athena, swifter than Mercury,
sifter of truths with a whip at my hip.
I've the cunning of an asp in my wink.

Advocate of sexual equality,
faster than a wasp, I type over
160 words a minute, given enough ink.

Frida Kahlo's Eyebrows

Born of glabella bushy as the pines, ever
as the firs, an all-encompassing embrace—
this is where the universe expands.

Below a hatful of bunched flowers, I motion
with her surly looks. I crease in all her pins
and blow on all her fires. Hateful? Trust me,

I've borne the wrath, the spars, the pity,
the truest emotion with quiet expression.
Crowd in to see the gleam of bat wings.

Full-crowed, my furrowed ebony elopes
with all the feelings that she flings. I angle
when the past aches in her bony bones. Though

people pluck my kind in two, my fate is unity.
I keep out the rains. Now keep up your chins.
Eyes like sparkly geodes, brows like gods—

without the piety. Browse the rest, the lops of vines,
the clips in the flesh, the ripe guts, the candied lips,
the braids, the cast of paste and gauze, the broken

spine, her necklace-wreath of thorns, the horde
of monkeys, the glam, the rip in her Tehuana dress
where a heart should be, like a hart's antlers gored her.

Let's be candid, my plumes eclipse them all.
Surely, I'm bold against her skin of beige.
I spin the world. So twirl your tongue of plums,

of pomegranate, and say what you would of my ego.
Go ahead and plant your big fat kisses here—
I'm the most beautiful thing on the planet.

On J

J is for jape. Ass-eared, I ape your pains.
My motley jangles. From certain angles,

ocular tricks turn these bells to jewels.
Dear Judy, love, stay jocular. We're pliable as jam,

though I am stuck. My jowl forever set, a curve
like the owl swoop, umbrella handles,

thing that yanks me by the neck, off stage,
injured, slack-jawed, continually awed.

I jounce and dance, one ounce
of iffy god in me, the rest galumphing otter,

inured to the joust. Don't cross me.
I'll oust the jovial professor in me in a jiffy.

The hand that makes me cruel. Jotter of jokes,
you poke and stir. Do not take me for a fool.

On Q-Tips

Dear Faqir,
I acquit you of any fakery
as a seed quickens into a mango tree
at your feet. It's a fair trick.

My acuity is cotton.
The q-tip is a qi caught in the ear
that stirs the qis, grown rotten,
matted like the sheep's coat

bedizened in suint. If I squint,
I see a tree of squandered
buds, bound for eyelids, bath tile, hindered
by warning, drowned in paint:

"Do not insert swab into ear canal."
As on a bed of spikes, pain is banal.

On D

"A few cubicles away a mild, ineffectual, dreamy creature named Ampleforth, with very hairy ears and a surprising talent for juggling with rhymes and metres, was engaged in producing garbled versions – definitive texts, they were called – of poems." – *1984*

D is for dark, although the ark of my mind rifts
with light streamed dearly on my face. It's early.

Day drifts in. I dwell in well-lit memory, in fire.
Reams of burning paper rile my dreams.

I sift through dust to find a rhyme for "rod."
Disintegrated words, just powder, riddled still

with power, float in a pale river of ash.
I had to go with *God*, for Kipling's sake!

Tie down the tide, drain the sea, paddle through
the muddle, obdurate as a mule. Fish for cod

with that damned *rod*. Redact and then react.
It's all the past. In the midst of this mist, I meander

through my cell and the mind's meaner deceits.
I see a cadre of discarded cares, regrets, of *dids*

and *hads*, the seed of *shoulds* and *woulds* that dash
the silence, drum the delicate alliance

between danger and anger. I grapple with time,
desiring dalliance, a bit of rum, and a sun-dappled apple.

On F

> "It seems that I must do a nude. All right, I'm going to do them a nude …" – Eduoard Manet

F as in Frank. I rank among the famous beauties,
Manet's *Olympia*, Victorine. My flame of copper hair,

in flakes of paint. Those lakes of paint I swam in once
when I set aside my robe of gold lamé to become a nude.

Flatter my eyes, sir, little glasses of cognac. The latter
is pure artifice. At the salon, I made every man fevery.

They grew flush. Called me a lush. How dare I stare?
My rule of thumb: If I ruffle feathers, you must be a peacock.

I caught flack because I lack the shyness of coquettes.
Once the frigid flock of spectators locked eyes on me,

they grew rigid, riled and rifled, flicked sticks at me,
licked their lips and yelled, *Grotesque!*

Olympia, my fable, my foil in oil, the goddess in me,
the flint on which to strike a fire, hangs in the exhibition hall.

Outside, I'm an able beggar and I beg your ire, my pockets
full of lint. I grow old and fold like a piece of canvas.

On Z

(Henrietta Lacks)

I'm like that zany jellyfish that never dies.
I've zigzagged the globe, prized

for the cells pried from my body, each
a fried egg, frizzed into multiple me's in Petri's.

My cervix, the color of rose quartz,
contained my children, cancer, a quart

of immortality, shiny and purple. Sift the Zion
of cells grown coy and cozy in my abdomen.

They burnt me black as tar; zoom in.
Take a look. The tzar that ruled me spread

like furzy with a fury. Life fizzled away;
the doctor filed my cells in the freezer. Zombie-me.

The afterlife is hazy, quick flashes in a zoetrope.
I remember I lay on the hay in a barn,

a lazy jazzy tune, the blues and the blue jay,
momentary things—the dazzle of light

on the ice-glazed dale. I doze off, doe-eyed,
milk the cows and clone the sheep. The frail river

of time collects frazil crystals, or runs drily, until
once again the world, full of zeal, becomes drizzly.

III

Derrida Eats a Dorito

To hold a Dorito is a venture toward the unpredictable.
The Dorito is neither this nor that, neither arrow
nor pyramid, neither scapula nor spandrel,
neither balalaika nor mythic dragon's breath,
neither inside my mouth nor outside,
neither revolution nor bowling pin formation,
neither a main course nor a discourse.

For what is *sapient* in this case
is to know a fiction, an angle, a cloak, a cheese—
the tick at which night touches day,
in lingering orange and little bits of gold.

Aristotle said brutes swallow; humans savor.
Whether I take or partake of the speckled disorder,
tornado in a bag, lost in its delta and sediment,
from the moment I open my mouth
I have already promised; or rather, and sooner,
the promise has seized the *I* which promises
to eat the Dorito.

Nothing Rhymes with Gitmo

The monoglot might slip on *guano-
toh-moh*. You tell dogs *git*, and gung-ho
handy types'll git her done.
Git mo' for less. As slick as a Ginsu
we nick up names and butcher lingo.
The foreign sounds familiar, Gringo.

It's our pet name, a Geico gecko
or a Tamagachi gizmo,
our little pal, the tickle-me-Gitmo,
as common as your local Citgo.
We quickly fill the Winnebago
and sort the *Logos* from the logo.

A nimble moniker suited FloJo,
her name and legs, a quick glissando.
Consider celebrity: our Hojo,
J-Lo, Brangelina, Brando—
abstract concepts, magnificos.
Much too grand, their names are name-brands.

Consider the word *snafu*, like Garbo,
delicate, posh, a slight *faux pas*.
The war-born acrimony, acro-
nymed, gets lost to sound bite, footnote,
shortcut, whatnot. Charlie, Pinko,
Jerry. Consider how the Gingko

tree, botanical dynamo,
survived a bombed Hiroshima.
A hail of syllables can hit
like bullets on Geronimo.
Language survives this way. Now,
enunciate. *Guantánamo*.

Keys to the Kingdom

Arks won't hold them. The creatures don't fit in, all hybrid ersatz beasts. The mule comes out smarter than his mom, still horsily, crossbred. How much smarts did his jackass father put in the mix? Domesticated cows succumb to buffalo. Mistake? No. Raw evolution? No. They're bred for beef, for cattalo, a kind of improv foisted upon them, to make a beefalo, a pitiful portmanteau. Gather tigers, leopards, jaguars, and lions; mix together and get hodgepodge spots and stripes, larger ligers, leopons, jaglions infused with a jack-a-dandied flair of fur and a new strange roar. Jungles grow jumbled, a mish-mashed Eden (modern day Iraq). Keepers of horses rope off their zebras before they get mixed up. Look at the zeehorse when…is it the hokey pokey that they do? Maybe we'll need a new breed of zebroid jockey. In addition, no one fathoms how a dolphin & whale make a wolphin. A whim obviously. A camel/llama combo makes a cama, not a llamel. Perhaps those hypoallergenic cats, customized in white and black queued up in biotechnology factory lines somewhere in NJ, really are ocecats primed to destroy your carpet. Would Gandhi support this? Should we consider the dogote as a pet? Or cherish the wily pet dox? What if the coydingo, coywolf, or coydog unleashed from doghouse to the wild, aren't coy at all? What if variety in life gets too spicy? What if the lion & dove make love? What if the turkey & mallard make malarkey, or we combined xenogenetic hippogriffs, harpies, mermaids, geep, exotic yakalo & pumapards? Name them watchmacalit, thingamabob? Zedonks, zebronkeys, Debra: pull your carts across Arcadia.

Albanian Virgin

I taped my breasts down; it was livable.
Once sworn to be a man, I bade farewell
to *doll, babe, cupcake, cutie, butterfly*,
and *daughter*, glittering necklaces, clitoris, labia,
rubies, nylons, silken dresses, lipstick,
everything that made me beautiful.
I'd be man-made. But my skin hurt, a lobster
red, a waste of tape. I stopped, soon baffled
that everyone, as if in a blindfold,
pretended my breasts disappeared, unlabeled
lumps under my suit jacket, more befitting
heavyset old men. I learned by heart
the lumbered movements of a man. I labored
over footsteps, feeling suddenly limbless,
hung upside down from the hard oak, limbered
my legs, my spine (for height), always barefoot,
my shoe-size rare. No one called my bluff.
No one. I puffed cigars, dispelled a labyrinth
of smoke, made women blush, but with no libido
for their soft shapes, I resented any lovebirds,
odd man out, and played the celibate bedfellow
of responsibility. Lifeless, breathful,
I spoke with a low voice, hoarse beefeater,
the son my parents never bottle-fed.
The house expenses (we're rich as butterfat)
I managed well, the business, those elaborate
dinner parties, hosting guests on behalf
of my proud family. But the blood feuds
did me in, made my home a battlefield.
Could I cry? Should I be bulletproof?
Be and *kill a man*, is this liberating?

The Snows of Kilimanjaro Are Melting

(after Hemingway)

The thing is painless when it starts. The big
birds squat obscenely, filthy, naked. Notice
them, minute against a herd of zebra
where sand grouse flighted in the mornings. Out
the window: snow on mountains, snow so bright
it hurt your eyes, sleigh-smoothed, cake frosting light
as powder. You dropped down, snow-bound, on crust.
You kept from thinking; it was marvelous.
This life of pleasant surrender was going with
a rush of water. A sudden emptiness
slipped lightly along the edge of the cool night.
The madness was a puff of wind that makes
a candle flicker and the flame go tall,
whispers that you did not hear, the ashes
shade would fish through. Morning blushed
and laughed with shortening hours. Death in pairs,
on bicycles, moved shy as deer, the dark
holding all the stories. Everything
you do, you do too long, and do too late.
Dying, as everything else, it's a bore. Death
can be a bird, or a wide snout hyena,
or simply occupied space, burning brightly,
waving to the zebra, the wildebeest.
Sculptured hollows sifting a blizzard from nowhere
seemed wide as all the world, as the square top
of Kilimanjaro stirred uneasily.

Windmills

Time reverses.
Old ladies trade their handbags in for smaller purses.
Little kids unlearn their curses.

The air grows cooler, clearer with the years. We drive
on highways, watching the wind in the windmills thrive,
feeling sun-plunged and alive.

The wind here rotates—gusts, then still.
The worn down right-side railroad track collects a metal particle.
We know the dug out side of the riverbed will fill.

We watch the windmills change. Ice-blue turbines sprout
more arms, propeller-like, gleaming sabers whirling about.
Giant silver sunflowers keep coming out.

The Dutch grow stone hut towers.
Rotten fruit grows ripe. Withered flowers
grow greener in the hours.

The raindrops compose, collecting shards.
They jump on cue towards
the sky as the windmills turn the world, then turn backwards.

Echo and Narcissus

I. Echo Goes Spelunking

She wants to say the word *spelunk*
to drink
its sound and pour it from her mouth
like myth.
The flashlight at her forehead glows
haloes.
She feels like the shadows on the wall,
so small.
Bats flap. Is her mud-covered skin
this thin?
She rappels deeper into mud.
Thud. "Thud."

II. Narcissus and Saran Wrap

Glimpsing the cling-wrapped bowl, Narcissus stands
before a blurry lover. Could it be real?
The fraction of mirror
couldn't be clearer.
He plunges lusty fingers in the seal.
The doting lover sucks and kisses his hands.

How suffocating though. He **NOW SEALS TIGHTER!**
with arms so crystal polyethylene,
so **Easy to Handle.**
And what a scandal
every steamy microwave-safe sex scene
becomes. And the lost love when lights get brighter.

Echo and Narcissus

III. Narcissus, Echo, and the Recycling Center

Through lines of plastic, the garbage, he says,
"Savor the rows where the offal brews."
Reflective bottles don't compare
to that mirror pool of Ancient Greece.

"Save her, the rose. Wear the awful bruise,"
she answers self-reflectively
to that mirror pool of ancient grease
dammed in the dirt road parking lot.

She answers self-reflectively
in a mud-puddled way, *Why me?*
Damned in the dirt road parking lot
to restate his words. As his face reflects

in the mud-puddled way, "Why me!"
He points, "No, he's a little meatier."
To restate his words, as his face reflects,
"No, maybe he's a little bolder."

She points. "No, he's a little meteor,"
she argues insufficiently.
"No, maybe he's a little boulder."
Annoyed, "Try speaking to your lyre," he retorts.

She argues insufficiently.
"You can't change chance," he says.
Annoyed, "Try speaking to *your* liar," she retorts.
He doesn't know how it feels to love.

Echo and Narcissus

"You can't change chants," she says.
Through lines of plastic—the garbage he says—
he doesn't know how it feels. To love,
reflective bottles don't compare.

Lust

(after Berryman, "Dream Song 4")

Somehow he ordered a dessert for dinner,
Italian ice cream, which cakes his beard.
Twice,
girding his telescopes, I glanced his way
in hopes he might break the palaver, a dish—jar the others.
Glinting alongside my fork

my little wedding ring kept singing, sighing
We're in Versailles, with me in petticoats,
wax and pearl pins
in my hair, sculpted out of air, and he
(imagined) brilliance, suited, *Sir Dinner Date*,
our world, a table long.

One pot of coffee pours in two cups,
steaming, just his and mine, the drink some pope once called
the wine of what…*infidels*?
My napkin's caught fire. My torso disintegrates
into a mist of birds and smoke. Outside: the rain and leaves falling,
every weighted thing.

Couple On Display

No voices. Listen. Softly trace the blueprint
of their idle tête-à-tête. The couple

on display, framed in the café window,
becomes a vignette. His morning paper kowtows

to her until he snaps its spine back stiff,
his tango partner dipping gently, deftly.

Why, it takes all his focus, the day's affairs.
How can he maneuver, sip his coffee,

let it all slip his grasp, even whisper,
to look up past the full wingspan of newsprint?

Her hands, long-winded, pantomime a puzzle
towards the wood pulp of the daily news.

Biscotti's meant to be this delicate.
Perhaps it's fundamental. Love goes stale.

Perhaps there's nothing left to say. Her gestures,
unmoving. The air between them hangs austere.

Or maybe she just mouths the words, *sfumato*,
voiced inside the locked cage of her throat.

Watch how her earrings, made of abalone,
shake with emphasis when she says, *Honey?*

On Beauty

(Colgate-Palmolive Company Soap Ad circa 1958)

You're prettier than you think you are!
…And you can prove it with a Palmolive bar!
The blonde-haired blue-eyed avatar
from the soap ad says so. What a dish she is!
Secretarial cupcake! The 1950s
concept dressed in pink stands polished and pure.

Cleanliness is next to comeliness.
You're prettier than you think and *la promesse*
du bonheur awaits you in the sink. Unless…
we go back further—centuries—*pretty*
meaning *tricky*. You're trickier than you think!
…And you can prove it with a palm! Oh yes!

Try sleight of hand. Be cunning. Then, think *clean*.
You pretty mess! You dirty trickster! Scan
the mirror. You're prettier than you…And you
can prove that *pretty* is a state of mind.
Now kick the dirt in someone else's face
because: You're prettier!…And you can!

30-Second Spot

Red spaghetti sauce on the table linens?
Pomegranate seeds on your wedding dress?
Barbecue stains on your white muscle tee?
Cherries jubilee on your picnic sundress?
Transubstantiated blood on the altar cloth?
Were you slicing beets while in your underwear
and wiped your fuchsia hands on your tighty-whities?
Were you impersonating John Travolta,
suited disco white at a party, neglecting
to put down your merlot as you pointed to the sky?
Did someone give you a bloody message of payback,
a beloved horse head on your new satin sheets?
Do you find yourself yelling, *Out, damned spot?*
Use *Tide*.

Poet as Anticapitalist

(after Denise Duhamel & Sean Penn)

You're no hillbilly Jed Clampett, dear Brad Pitt.
He discovered a crude, bubbling serendipity
shooting rabbits out back as the ground spit
gold. But you know about coincidence, the pitfalls
of dating two celebrities at once, the pitchfork
crowd from that time you were a vampire, both decrepit

and pretty. Can you tell me why then, Brad Pitt,
in *Fight Club*, slippery as an avocado pit,
they showed a theater in the background and pitted
against the sky was a poster of a film starring Brad Pitt?
Why then did your cocky, fist-fighting anticapitalist
character sip beer then tell Edward Norton, low-pitched,

"What are we then? We're consumers," the recapitulation
of a statement you made while in a mental hospital
in *12 Monkeys,* ranting from your crazy-pulpit.
Brad, can I call you Brad? I work for a pittance;
you're filthy rich. If oil is capitalism,
poetry is water. They don't quite mix. The pitter-patter

of rain is free. A running tap, marked H&C, spits
the life-sustaining source and can fill a pitcher,
a tub, two-thirds a body, a poem. But capitalism
reigns the water on the island of Fiji, and muddies my pithy
metaphor for poetry a bit. The precipitation
there is still puddle-wonderful despite

the fact that Fiji's local tap water is a cesspit
and that the FIJI company's grip on the epitome
of bottled chic creates a bottomless pit
of plastic. Living in Fiji must be the pits.
But you can see how oil is worse. The turpitude
of war. The gulf spill. Where shall we dig next? Jupiter?

Poet as Anticapitalist

I know what you're thinking. Doesn't this Brad Pitt
poem, addressed to me, the illustrious Brad Pitt,
veer away from its subject? I could launch a spitball
at you, Brad. I know you've drunken FIJI water. A pity.
And every BP station shares your monogram, Pitt.
I'm not in love with you, Brad, you australopithecine.

IV

Tonight the Character of Death Will Be Played by Brad Pitt

Gentle reader, you are not Brad Pitt.
You're reading poetry and at this hour
Brad Pitt is likely not perusing poems
and certainly not this one. Therefore, you
are not Brad Pitt. You may be overweight,
less than gorgeous, wearing your pajamas,
and Brad Pitt's a lot more svelte than you
(and also better looking). But consider
for a moment if we skinned Brad Pitt,
as many may be loath or wont to do;
he would resemble the flayed muscleman
from a book of Renaissance anatomy,
De Humani Corporis Fabrica.
Fanciful drawings. For example, one
particular cadaver, let's call him Brad Pitt,
displays his muscles, prancing in a field.
That facial expression that Brad Pitt makes
is the same one you made today. In fact,
you share many muscles with Brad Pitt,
though his are surely bigger and more chiseled
than yours. Such bizarre drawings are a window.
It's how you know you have a spleen. One day,
that knowledge and Brad Pitt may save your life.

The Bar

A long, long time ago. I still remember how
we slogged past cold tall piles of the snow plow.
What was I—nine? The ski lodge serving wine,
the dance floor and the band we sat behind.

The karaoke Germans singing "Hard Day's Night,"
Oh nein! My mother tipsy next to me. That light,
its slant, the fireplace, the choice to sing—*her* style—
and maybe she was happy for a while,

pie-eyed, singing "Bye-Bye Miss American Pie."
It made us heavy with a bevy of eyes.
Even the hairy big-nosed moose heads stared at us,
both flashing through a pink-shade spectrum, faces blushed.

For her it was the fun; for me, the shame, the fuss.
I'd soon invent Embarrasser's Anonymous
and be a staunch teetotaler of ten
because of that refrain that came again, again.

Long song. The cocktail cherries found it a little wordy,
the words she forgot replaced with "Everybody!"
Bye Shirley, Mary, your bloody temple. Bye-bye
the thought that this would be the day I'd die.

Aubade for Resusci-Annie

She knelt beside the dummy head, said *Annie,*
Annie, are you okay? The school nurse breathed
a sigh. She'd dressed that morning close to dawn,
her stark white stockings laced with dust. Clear-eyed,
she demonstrated how to save a life.

My turn. I shook her arm, her plastic life,
held my ear to her lips, said *Annie, Annie,*
are you okay? The nurse kept vigil. I'd
recite the script of *look, listen, feel, breathe…*
as if she'd spark like tinder, wake like dawn.

I knew no history of a French dawn,
of "L'inconnue de la Seine," Jeanne Doe, whose life
expired in that river, whose final breath
of water told no story. Now she's Annie,
the model for this plastic face I eyed.

The Paris morgue attendant, starry-eyed,
had made her death mask—porcelain, calm, no dawn
in her cold cheeks. That face, soon found in any
souvenir shop, spends her 1980's afterlife
in matted hair, blue sweats, awaiting breath.

The rhythmic ritual of borrowed breath
has the faint look of love, a care conveyed.
But life-sized dolls can't bear the size of life.
That year, we were flooding, about to dawn.
We were too young. My first kiss was Annie.

Doll Coffins

The porcelain dolls lined up and laid on shelves
look staid collecting dust in the guest room.
Framed in cowls of curls, their faces loom,
almost alive again like little elves.

But I dig out their boxes from the attic,
check the numbers on their necks, then match
certificates to head molds, thumb a scratch,
untangle knots, smooth out each dress's static.

I feather dust from the blonde bangs and slide
a lacy hem, the faded corduroy,
the smooth cold skin inside her box—the toy
that can't be played with—eyes still opened wide.

The Fascist Poem

"The Fascist Poem, one may fear, will be a horrid little abortion such as one sees in a glass jar in the museum of some county town." – Virginia Woolf

Words won't form in my crooked mouth, a perfect
Red, a perfect message, a pitch too perfect.

Shelved. Scrunched in liquid, thighs to my neck, feet curled,
Both my faces pressed to glass make perfect

Wrinkles. Through the jar, the green world blurs,
Exhausts the muscles of my eyes, that perfect

View. The forest kaleidoscopes in fall,
Dropping flames. A woman strolls. A perfect

Day to clutch the little baby to her round
Little breast, that perfect piece of flesh, such perfect

Happiness. Splinters of truth in every lie
Float through the pristine air, collect in perfect

Bundles. One girl for every boy, chopping
Trees with muscle and ax, mechanical, as in perfect

Rhyme. The world spins. Hills. Vales. Dirt. Bone. A perfect
Circle. We cannot hope for a world more perfect.

Ode to Fear

Of atomic explosions. Of comets. Of ghosts.
Of chopsticks. Of paper. Of puppets. Of dust.

Of mountains. Of poison. Of failure. Of snow.
Of burglars. Of virgins. Of vertigo.

Of the figure eight. Of glass. Of floods.
Of moths. Of myths. Of thunder. Of crowds.

Of wrinkles. Of whirlpools. Of ruins. Of death.
Of tickling feathers. Of theatres. Of teeth.

Of birds. Of beards. Of wind. Of string.
Of pins and needles. Of swallowing.

Of dentists. Of dolls. Of clowns. Of coitus.
Of crossing bridges. Of love. Of loud noises.

Of bicycles. Of flutes. Of tyrants. Of heights.
Of flying. Of fire. Of forests at night.

Of blushing. Of sharks. Of the crucifix.
Of belly buttons. Of Bolsheviks.

Of double vision. Of pleasure. Of the sea.
Of memories. Of mere being. Of bees.

Battle of the Cricket

Atop the doorknob
throbs a hopper,
a camel cricket
stuck like enamel,
blocking my path.
Breathless, spooked,
the face of a devil
cleaves much too close—
I can't touch the door.
He's sure to sprint in,
toading all over,
roving my abode.
I throw small rocks.
Lax and stoic,
he lingers on the knob,
grubby king,
ghastly dragon,
haggard bastard.
He's not at all
the small, hideous
reincarnation
flesh-again-view
of my grandfather.
Unearthing bravery,
I advance to the door.
In a blur, we dance,
striding, then skipping,
jumping side to side,
as he welcomes, faint-hearted,
his partner, screaming.

Textbook Smile

The flayed head illustrated here is like the sun.
He's solitary, round, and his half-shut eyes shine,
although his lips are dun. A coral cord is spun
across his hairless, skinless head like sticky twine.

All roses tint the layers of his muscled cheek,
petals in cut reflected flaps, striated red.
Methyl alcohol on his lack of breath must reek,
but I smell nothing, touch smooth paper, lay my head

beside his on my book. I study his face to find,
through his *risorius* and *masseter*, just how
his smile rises, falls, just where his teeth would grind,
and how a feeling comes across his vacant brow.

And when he smiles, yes, it's something like the sun.
My wayward Latinate lover smiles at everyone.

Graven Image

(after Vesalius)

We must not think about the soft carved neck
of a fat turkey or the brilliant pink
and red in butcher shops, all chockablock.
We must not think
about the skin-scraped knee or the last blink
we'll take. You see the trick of the woodblock;
the wood's been carved, not skin; the blood is ink,
stark black, not the gray form that the dead take.
But a man's hand cut heart, cut skull, the clink
of bone like God conceived at daylight's break.
We must not think.

Noli Me Tangere

"Touch isn't clear…it's…inapparent, obscure, secret, nocturnal."
– Aristotle (translated by Derrida)

A paper pink
umbrella sits inside a cocktail drink
and shades a maraschino from the sun.

The winds pick up.
Your skin perks, comprehending the cool hiccup
as the contrast of the shadows fade.

If I simply
look at the delicate *impatiens*, limply
jeweled with rain, repelling little beads,

their seed sacks burst
into tiny folded fans. They're cursed
to isolation, fragrant at this distance.

My umbrella
handle reads J. A clear defined penumbra
marks the air where only shade can touch me.

Light thuds of rain
reverberate through metal, plastic, skin
and bone. To utter is to touch upon,

how a whisper
grasps the ear, the touch of heat, a vesper.
My outstretched hand collects the licks of rain.

If a stranger
nears me, teases my hair as his fingers
trace my spine, we never really touch.

Noli Me Tangere

Asymptotic,
our atoms mingle, or we trade a static
charge, or dance in an alternate universe.

The rain's presence—
shattering, is also a disappearance.
Small gems of it form rivers, hide in tree roots.

Stranger beware.
I've already left. I am no longer where
I am. I am no longer who I am.

Eurydice

So this is hell—like tasteless lemonade.
Unraveling the sugar shell, each shade…
well…everybody's boring as cement.
But I'm not bitter—I'm dull too. The scent
of water's in the air. Our talk's clichéd.
We all play dead. The flowers are decayed.
If I could be a gazelle, afraid…or filleted
in bright hellfire…how my thoughts ferment
so! This is hell—

because my mind won't change it. Synapse frayed,
eye coins spent, my mind will fade and fade.
I'm like a butter knife and I'm hell bent
on apathy. Even his last look meant
nothing—another feckless promenade.
So this is hell.

My Sexist Thesaurus

Rubens' *Venus* must have a body mass index
higher than 25. A pot-belly pouch
and fleshy legs. It's Venus in cellulite.
But how do I describe her lack of fig leaves?
A swath of cloth hides the nothingness between
her legs. While my thesaurus is aware
of genitalia, pudenda, private parts,
it cannot name a part specifically,

except for *family jewels*. Adonis sits there,
male: bold, strapping, sturdy, virile, robust.
Husky, macho gallant gorilla-beefcake.
My thesaurus lacks political correctness.
No penis, nor vagina. No *ass,* just *butt,*
meaning *ram*, *clay pigeon*, and *cigarette*.

Female, girl, shrew, changeable she-devil,
fishwife, fair virgin/vixen, tender temptress
in petticoats. How not to offend? Fertility
organs? Delicate pin-up lady parts?
Or effete flower where the sun don't shine?

Emaciated Muse

Her face, framed in despair, osteocyte
on osteocyte, starves. Her mouth won't bite.
Her strigiform, wise eyes come out of night
soaked to the lacrimal bones.
One foot
holds all her weight (not much). She'll put
air in your throat, humerus tones,
as she elbows you in the gut.

Descartes' seat of the soul rests near the lap's
design of a white Turkish saddle that straps
the bat within her skull. You speak; it flaps.
Sinister pairs of snakes bite
the line
of vertebrae bumped down her spine,
and curve in a cage of yellowish white
each time you don't quite rhyme.

Her ringed torso, a frail rattling trill,
clinks her iliac crest, her limbs. They spill
from cranium to toe to the floor until
from fossae to trochleas,
she sings;
her scapulas are angel's wings.
She spirals in your cochleas
and with honeydew she stings.

Harpy

If I spoke *English*, I'd say, "Look at that hot bird"
and I'd mean *girl*, the one with wings and a bright fantail
who blew in like the wind from somewhere so absurd
you couldn't say whether weather was the guilty gale
that swept her here. She's hungry for something, manic, mannish,
tearing at the world like a kid at a candy wrapper.
What is that otherworldly shrieking? What shrill shrew?
She's looking. Look into her steely eyes and vanish—
she's scratching you. If I had a girl like that, I'd slap her
on a Grecian urn and tell her she's beautiful, it's true.

Still Life

When they unearthed my body, I was precious,
not for my pretty sapphires, which I lacked,
but because life lay still in me. Precautions
were taken to keep me there; I'd been locked,
this form in a coffin, but I'd been licked
and pried open. Theirs was a loathsome practice,
I thought, burgling the dead to steal peace.
I'd rot soon enough without some precocious
anatomist cutting me up to display me on his lectern.
This man walked the length of my hand, punctured
my skin, hurried down to the quiet heart, located
my female parts. He emptied me like a pitcher,
a pretty little teapot, pretty as a picture.
His hands began to map a chart of living, looked
through me, learning, while my insides leaked out.
He arranged my organs like fruit in a dish, all pinkish,
sketched me quickly. Now my body lies likened
in a manuscript. I'd lived on. I'd lucked out.
What great things I could do besides perish.

Notes

TITLE: "'Comment ne pas dire…?' The use of the French word *dire* permits a certain suspension. 'Comment ne pas dire?' can mean, in a manner that is both transitive and intransitive, how to be silent, how not to speak in general, how to avoid speaking? But it can also mean: how, in speaking, not to say this or that, in this or that manner? In other words: how, in saying and speaking, to avoid this or that discursive, logical, rhetorical mode? How to avoid an inexact, erroneous, aberrant, improper form? How to avoid such a predicate, and even predication itself? For example: how to avoid a negative form, or how not to be negative? Finally, how to say something?" – Derrida on the selection of his title, "How to Avoid Speaking."

SYNAESTHESIA modifies a quote by Pierre Bonnard: "I've discovered peaches. They're so intense and soft, and some of them resemble a setting sun," as quoted in *Bonnard and His Environment*. This poem takes as its subject the theory of Daphne Maurer and Charles Maurer (*The World of the Newborn*) that proposes all infants are synaesthetic – a phenomenon that is lost over time through a process of neural pruning.

SAXIFRAGE IS MY FLOWER THAT SPLITS THE ROCKS takes its title from the William Carlos Williams poem "A Sort of Song."

HOW TO AVOID SPEAKING shares its title with a lecture by Derrida from which the following phrases are adapted: "nebulous multiplicity of potentials," and "You affirm nothing."

ANDY WARHOL'S WIG owes much of its understanding of Andy Warhol's body image issues to *The Hypochondriacs: Nine Tormented Lives*.

ON D references the obscure character Ampleforth in Orwell's *1984*: "'We were producing a definitive edition of the poems of Kipling. I allowed the word "God" to remain at the end of a line. I could not help it!' he added almost indignantly, raising his face to look at Winston. 'It was impossible to change the line. The rhyme was "rod". Do you realize that there are only twelve rhymes to "rod" in the entire language?'"

ON F: Victorine Meurent's eyes were described as "little glasses of cognac" by art historian George Moore, as quoted in *Alias Olympia*, which also

Notes

provides the biographical understanding for this poem.

ON Z owes its understanding of the biography of Henrietta Lacks to *The Immortal Life of Henrietta Lacks*.

DERRIDA EATS A DORITO adapts a passage from Derrida's essay "How to Avoid Speaking: Denials" quoting specifically "X is neither this nor that, neither the contrary of this nor of that, neither the simple neutralization of this nor of that…" and "From the moment I open my mouth I have already promised; or rather, and sooner the promise has seized the *I* which promises to speak to the other, to say something…"

KEYS TO THE KINGDOM owes its form to Barbara Hamby—modeled after her double-helix abecedarian and abecedarian sonnets employed in *The All-Night Lingo Tango*.

THE SNOWS OF KILIMANJARO ARE MELTING is a kind of erasure poem, built of Hemingway's phrases, and altering some, melting most of the story's words away.

30-SECOND SPOT modifies an advertisement, as quoted in *The Language Instinct* by Steven Pinker. "Cherries jubilee on a white suit? Wine on an altar cloth? Apply club soda immediately. It works beautifully to remove the stains from fabrics."

POET AS ANTICAPITALIST owes its form, the mock sestina, each line ending in a Pitt variant, to Denise Duhamel's poem "Delta Flight 659" addressed to Sean Penn, a "mock sestina, each line ending in a Penn variant."

EMACIATED MUSE: Descartes regarded the pineal gland as the seat of the soul. Nearby sits another seat, the *sella turcica*, or "Turkish saddle," a depression in the sphenoid bone (a skull bone shaped like a bat) that cradles the pituitary gland. Both glands are located in the epithalamus of the brain.

A Note About the Author

Jaimee Hills was born in Plainfield, New Jersey, in 1979 and was educated at the Johns Hopkins University and the University of North Carolina at Greensboro. Her poems have appeared in *Best New Poets, Measure, Blackbird*, and elsewhere. She is the author of *How to Avoid Speaking*, winner of the 2014 Anthony Hecht Poetry Prize. She currently teaches in the English department at Marquette University and lives with her husband, Gerry Canavan, and their two children in Milwaukee, Wisconsin.

A Note About the Anthony Hecht Poetry Prize

The Anthony Hecht Poetry Prize was inaugurated in 2005 and is awarded on an annual basis to the best first or second collection of poems submitted.

FIRST ANNUAL HECHT PRIZE
Judge: J. D. McClatchy
Winner: Morrie Creech, *Field Knowledge*

SECOND ANNUAL HECHT PRIZE
Judge: Mary Jo Salter
Winner: Erica Dawson, *Big-Eyed Afraid*

THIRD ANNUAL HECHT PRIZE
Judge: Richard Wilbur
Winner: Rose Kelleher, *Bundle o' Tinder*

FOURTH ANNUAL HECHT PRIZE
Judge: Alan Shapiro
Winner: Carrie Jerrell, *After the Revival*

FIFTH ANNUAL HECHT PRIZE
Judge: Rosanna Warren
Winner: Matthew Ladd, *The Book of Emblems*

SIXTH ANNUAL HECHT PRIZE
Judge: James Fenton
Winner: Mark Kraushaar, *The Uncertainty Principle*

SEVENTH ANNUAL HECHT PRIZE
Judge: Mark Strand
Winner: Chris Andrews, *Lime Green Chair*

EIGHTH ANNUAL HECHT PRIZE
Judge: Charles Simic
Winner: Shelley Puhak, *Guinevere in Baltimore*

A Note About the Anthony Hecht Poetry Prize

Ninth Annual Hecht Prize
Judge: Heather McHugh
Winner: Geoffrey Brock, *Voices Bright Flags*

Tenth Annual Hecht Prize
Judge: Anthony Thwaite
Winner: Jaimee Hills, *How to Avoid Speaking*

For further information, please visit Waywiser's website at

http://waywiser-press.com/hechtprize.html

Other Books from Waywiser

POETRY
Al Alvarez, *New & Selected Poems*
Chris Andrews, *Lime Green Chair*
George Bradley, *A Few of Her Secrets*
Geoffrey Brock, *Voices Bright Flags*
Robert Conquest, *Blokelore & Blokesongs*
Robert Conquest, *Penultimata*
Morri Creech, *Field Knowledge*
Morri Creech, *The Sleep of Reason*
Peter Dale, *One Another*
Erica Dawson, *Big-Eyed Afraid*
B. H. Fairchild, *The Art of the Lathe*
David Ferry, *On This Side of the River: Selected Poems*
Jeffrey Harrison, *The Names of Things: New & Selected Poems*
Joseph Harrison, *Identity Theft*
Joseph Harrison, *Shakespeare's Horse*
Joseph Harrison, *Someone Else's Name*
Joseph Harrison, ed., *The Hecht Prize Anthology, 2005-2009*
Anthony Hecht, *Collected Later Poems*
Anthony Hecht, *The Darkness and the Light*
Carrie Jerrell, *After the Revival*
Stephen Kampa, *Bachelor Pad*
Rose Kelleher, *Bundle o' Tinder*
Mark Kraushaar, *The Uncertainty Principle*
Matthew Ladd, *The Book of Emblems*
Dora Malech, *Shore Ordered Ocean*
Jérôme Luc Martin: *The Gardening Fires: Sonnets and Fragments*
Eric McHenry, *Potscrubber Lullabies*
Eric McHenry and Nicholas Garland, *Mommy Daddy Evan Sage*
Timothy Murphy, *Very Far North*
Ian Parks, *Shell Island*
V. Penelope Pelizzon, *Whose Flesh is Flame, Whose Bone is Time*
Chris Preddle, *Cattle Console Him*
Shelley Puhak, *Guinevere in Baltimore*
Christopher Ricks, ed., *Joining Music with Reason:
34 Poets, British and American, Oxford 2004-2009*
Daniel Rifenburgh, *Advent*
Mary Jo Salter, *It's Hard to Say: Selected Poems*
W. D. Snodgrass, *Not for Specialists: New & Selected Poems*
Mark Strand, *Almost Invisible*
Mark Strand, *Blizzard of One*
Bradford Gray Telford, *Perfect Hurt*
Matthew Thorburn, *This Time Tomorrow*

Other Books from Waywiser

Cody Walker, *Shuffle and Breakdown*
Deborah Warren, *The Size of Happiness*
Clive Watkins, *Already the Flames*
Clive Watkins, *Jigsaw*
Richard Wilbur, *Anterooms*
Richard Wilbur, *Mayflies*
Richard Wilbur, *Collected Poems 1943-2004*
Norman Williams, *One Unblinking Eye*
Greg Williamson, *A Most Marvelous Piece of Luck*
Greg Williamson: *The Hole Story of Kirby the Sneak and Arlo the True*

FICTION
Gregory Heath, *The Entire Animal*
Mary Elizabeth Pope, *Divining Venus*
K. M. Ross, *The Blinding Walk*
Gabriel Roth, *The Unknowns**
Matthew Yorke, *Chancing It*

ILLUSTRATED
Nicholas Garland, *I wish ...*
Eric McHenry and Nicholas Garland, *Mommy Daddy Evan Sage*
Greg Williamson: *The Hole Story of Kirby the Sneak and Arlo the True*

NON-FICTION
Neil Berry, *Articles of Faith: The Story of British Intellectual Journalism*
Mark Ford, *A Driftwood Altar: Essays and Reviews*
Richard Wollheim, *Germs: A Memoir of Childhood*

* Co-published with Picador